ALEXANDER MORRIS

Finding Balance in the Chaos

"Yoga Techniques for Mindful Living. A Relaxing Story of Transformation & Self Discovery

First published by Alexander Morris 2024

Copyright © 2024 by Alexander Morris

All rights reserved. No part of this publication may be reproduced, stored or transmitted in any form or by any means, electronic, mechanical, photocopying, recording, scanning, or otherwise without written permission from the publisher. It is illegal to copy this book, post it to a website, or distribute it by any other means without permission.

This novel is entirely a work of fiction. The names, characters and incidents portrayed in it are the work of the author's imagination. Any resemblance to actual persons, living or dead, events or localities is entirely coincidental.

Alexander Morris asserts the moral right to be identified as the author of this work.

Alexander Morris has no responsibility for the persistence or accuracy of URLs for external or third-party Internet Websites referred to in this publication and does not guarantee that any content on such Websites is, or will remain, accurate or appropriate.

Designations used by companies to distinguish their products are often claimed as trademarks. All brand names and product names used in this book and on its cover are trade names, service marks, trademarks and registered trademarks of their respective owners. The publishers and the book are not associated with any product or vendor mentioned in this book. None of the companies referenced within the book have endorsed the book.

First edition

This book was professionally typeset on Reedsy.
Find out more at reedsy.com

To those who have ever felt like they were drowning on the inside

Contents

Foreword — ii
Acknowledgments — iii
1 The Struggle is Real — 1
2 Aftermath — 8
3 Sage of Wonder — 12
4 Flashing Intuition — 21
5 Awakening — 25
6 Morning Ritual — 28
7 Embracing Change — 32
8 Power of Observation — 35
9 Shifting Perspectives — 38
10 A Chance Encounter — 42
11 The Journey Within — 44
12 The Stone and the Sand — 48
13 Inner Radiance — 51
14 The Unraveling — 54
15 Guiding Spirit — 57
Afterword — 62

Foreword

Writing this book has been a joyful and transformative experience for me, inspired by the collective wisdom of authors, yogis, friends, and some of my own life experiences.

Through Devan's journey, I've woven in elements of self-discovery and resilience, illustrating how one man's awakening can resonate and inspire others to seek balance and purpose amid chaos.

This book aims to provide thoughtful reflections and gentle reminders, leaving you with a sense of connection and inspiration to share with those you care about.

In Finding Balance in the Chaos, the narrative goes beyond storytelling to reveal practical meditations and practices that can significantly enhance our overall quality of life.

As Devan embarks on his journey, he discovers techniques that help him feel more grounded and present, allowing readers to explore these same methods for themselves.

By incorporating these practices, you'll find tools to navigate challenges with greater ease and cultivate a sense of inner peace.

Acknowledgments

- The Celestine Prophecy by Robert Redford
- Untethered Soul by Michael Singer
- Creative Visualization by Shakti Gawain
- Men are from Mars Women are from Venus by John Grey
- Exploring the World of Lucid Dreaming Stephen LaBerge & Howard Rheingold
- Make Your Bed by William H. McRaven
- All of my fellow Yogis, Yoginies, Teacher, Students and Family

1

The Struggle is Real

You know that feeling when you hit snooze on your alarm, telling yourself, *"Five more minutes, that's all I need,"* but somehow you wake up two hours later, and the only reason you even open your eyes is because the sunlight's blasting through the window like a prison spotlight, you're late for work and you've barely enough time to get your pants on rushing out the door forgetting your keys, phone and wallet? Yeah, that's pretty much my life. We're not in highschool anymore. There are no teachers chasing me through the halls. I have an email inbox full of passive-aggressive "reminders" and a girlfriend who's started giving me that look. You know the one—the *"how much longer am I putting up with this?"* look.

Oh, where are my manners? Name's Devan. Devan Wilder. Some people call me a slacker; I prefer to think of myself as an "efficiency enthusiast." If something can be done in 20 minutes, why spend an hour? And if it doesn't really need to get done, well... why do it at all?

I've always been a fan of shortcuts, but lately, it's starting to feel like I'm cutting corners on my own life. It's weird—no one tells you that skipping through adulthood is different than skipping high school. Back then, I could sweet-talk my way out of anything: late assignments, missed classes, you name it. But now? Now it's like every task that's thrown at me just gets stacked up into a jenga tower of stress, ready to topple on my head at any moment.

Take work, for example. I'm an investigative journalist for a well-known magazine, the kind of publication with enough prestige to make my mom brag about it to her book club. But honestly? The job feels beneath me. Half the time, I'm chasing down puff pieces or "exclusive" stories that aren't exactly Pulitzer material. I mean, I got into this game to dig into the truth, to break real stories, not to churn out clickbait that barely scratches the surface.

It's not hard work, but that's the problem—it's almost *too* easy. I can knock out a piece in my sleep, which, frankly, I sometimes do. The challenge, if you can call it that, is pretending to care about it long enough to hit my word count. The grind is endless, sure, but there's no thrill, no payoff. It feels like I'm running on autopilot, and my talent's rusting away because the job doesn't even ask for half of it. So yeah, I slack off. It's hard to stay motivated when you know you're capable of so much more, but no one's asking for it.

Emails, editorial deadlines, article revisions, and a barrage of team notifications I navigate like I'm playing a high-stakes survival game. It's ridiculous how good I've gotten at avoiding direct interaction—it's almost a reflex now. My superpower, if you can call it that, is flying under the radar, ducking out of confrontation like my life depends on it. But that also means I can't bring myself to tell my boss the truth—that his constant "just checking in" emails make my skin crawl, like I'm being hunted, every ding setting off a fresh round of panic.

Instead, I fall back on what I've mastered over time: faking a smile, tapping keys aimlessly. Meanwhile, my mind drifts as I scroll through social media or pretend to be busy, hoping—maybe even praying— that today isn't the day someone notices I'm barely holding it together. There's this dull ache of helplessness creeping up on me, like I'm trapped in this endless loop of pretending to care about things that don't even matter.

The worst part? It's not the work itself—it's the sheer relentlessness of it, the suffocating feeling that no matter how hard I try, I'm always just one bad day away from completely unraveling. And deep down, I know if someone actually looked too closely, they'd see right through the act, see how close I am to breaking. But what can I do? So, I just keep faking it, because I don't know how to do anything else anymore.

But here's the kicker: I think my avoidance is starting to catch up with me. The other day I had to give a presentation. No big deal, right? Except, the night before, I found myself staring at the ceiling, frozen, trying to breathe like one of those yoga apps told me to. Spoiler alert: breathing doesn't solve everything. By the time the presentation came, I was sweating through my shirt and stumbling over words like a teenager asking their crush to prom. And let me tell you, that little flare-up of panic? Yeah, it stuck around. Suddenly, I'm questioning every email I send, every glance from my coworkers. Anxiety's got me in a chokehold, and the worst part is, I can't admit it to anyone. Not even my girlfriend, Maya.

Ah, Maya. She's kind, smart, and seems to have her life together, which makes me wonder what the hell she's doing with me. I used to think our dynamic worked because I brought the fun and spontaneity, and she kept us grounded. Lately though, fun has started to look more like flakiness. I come home late, mumble something about work, and she gives me this *look*. Not mad. Not even disappointed. Just... *tired*. And when Maya looks tired, I get worried. We've been together five years, and she's the real deal. The only thing holding me back from stepping it up is me.

I mean, don't get me wrong, it's not like I don't care. I care *a lot*. I just don't know how to fix this without putting in the kind of effort I've spent my whole life avoiding. I thought I could just keep coasting. But it turns out, ignoring your problems doesn't make them disappear—it makes them grow, fester even, like a forgotten pizza slice under the couch.

And then there's my family. My parents, still in the same house I grew up in, checking in on me with that mix of pride and concern. I was always "the golden child," the one who could charm his way through any situation. They don't see what's really happening—the constant pressure, the anxiety that hits like a freight train, the feeling that I'm one missed deadline away from everything crumbling. Or maybe they do, and they're just too polite to say anything.

Funny thing is, in high school, I could've gotten away with all of this. No one expected much back then—just a kid having a good time, figuring it out. Now though, the stakes are higher, and I'm not so sure the charm works anymore.

I think that's what's bugging me the most. I've spent so long skating by, thinking I could just outsmart life. But life's got a way of catching up to you, like an overdue bill, or a missed opportunity that you didn't even realize was knocking. The constant procrastination isn't just a quirk anymore—it's eating away at my confidence, my health, and every relationship I care about.

And the funny part? Even knowing all of that, I still can't seem to shake the habit. I keep telling myself that tomorrow is the day I'll pull it together. I'll answer those emails, prep for the meetings, finally have that tough conversation with my boss, and maybe even tell Maya what's really going on in my head.

But not today.

Today? I'm taking a long lunch.

Besides, this day has already gone off the rails, starting with Allen's public takedown in the morning meeting. He didn't even try to hide it, throwing me under the bus like it was a sport.

"Must be nice," Allen had said with a smirk, loud enough for the whole room to hear, "rolling in late every day, doing the bare minimum. I guess someone's gotta keep the seat warm while the rest of us actually work."

His words hit like a punch to the gut, and the room went awkwardly silent. Everyone knew Allen had it out for me, but no one ever stepped in. I felt the heat rise in my face, the mix of shame and anger making my heart race. I wanted to say something, anything to shut him up, but I just sat there, swallowing the words like poison. He grinned, knowing he'd gotten to me.

Instead of standing up for myself, I bit my tongue and let the meeting drag on, the tension thick enough to choke on. When it finally ended, I couldn't even think about heading home. Not with that humiliation hanging over me. So, I went to the one place where I didn't have to explain anything.

The bar. Rob, the bartender, didn't need to ask what I wanted—he already knew. He poured me a whiskey, then another, and I nursed the burn, letting it take the edge off the sting of Allen's words.

The whiskey went down smooth, but the bitter taste of the day still lingered, and as I sat there, staring into the glass, I couldn't shake the feeling that tomorrow was already slipping away too.

"Work stuff?" he asked, leaning on the counter.

"Something like that," I muttered, staring at the amber liquid. "Coworkers, man. They know just how to push your buttons. Today was pretty brutal."

"Only way it stops is if you stop it," he said, shrugging like it was the simplest thing in the world. "Don't let 'em get to you."

I forced a laugh. "Easier said than done."

I stayed longer than I should have, and when I finally got up to leave, I wasn't exactly steady. Stumbling out the door, I missed a step and went down hard, smacking my face against the pavement. I felt the warm trickle of blood before I even realized what had happened—a gash opening just above my cheekbone. It stung like hell, but not as much as the shame that followed. I was a hot mess.

Somehow, I dragged myself home, swiping the blood from my face with my sleeve. When I walked through the door, Maya was waiting. Her eyes widened as soon as she saw me.

"What the hell happened to your face!?" she shrieked, rushing over.

"I'm fine," I grumbled, brushing her off, already too exhausted to deal with it.

"Fine? You're bleeding!" grabbing a towel and pressing it against my cheek. "Where were you?"

"Out," I muttered, not looking at her.

"Out where? You didn't answer my texts."

"I was at the bar, Maya. What do you want me to say?"

She shook her head, frustration rising. "Don't shut me out. Every time things get hard, you disappear and leave me wondering."

I could feel the weight of her words, but I couldn't bring myself to engage. I was too tired, too numb. "I'm not disappearing. I just needed some time."

"Time for what? To drown your problems in whiskey?" Her voice cracked, a mix of anger and hurt. "You can't keep doing this, you know. Running away, shutting down. I'm here, but you're not."

I didn't have a good response. I didn't have *any* response. So I just stood there, cold and distant, knowing I was hurting her and somehow feeling powerless to stop.

Finally, she sighed, the fight leaving her. "I'm going to bed. I have an early day tomorrow."

"Yeah, me too," I replied flatly, avoiding her gaze as I turned and headed toward the couch.

I didn't press any further. I just grabbed a pillow and blanket, lying down on the couch while the gash on my face throbbed and the guilt building in my gut. I could hear her footsteps retreating to the bedroom, the door closing softly behind her.

As I stared at the ceiling, I felt the weight of everything pressing down on me. The work stress, the coworkers, the drinking, Maya—it hit me all at once and I wanted to scream but just swallowed hard. I knew the charm and excuses wouldn't be enough to dig me out of this hole.

2

Aftermath

The morning feels like it's crawling inside my skull, scraping against my brain with every pulse of my heartbeat. The hangover's no gentle wake-up call; it's more like a sledgehammer, relentless and punishing. My mouth is dry, my tongue thick like cotton, and my head pounds with a steady throb that makes the idea of even standing seem like too much effort.

The apartment is quiet, except for the low clink of dishes in the kitchen. I peel myself off the couch, every muscle aching, my joints stiff from a night spent curled in uncomfortable angles. The air smells faintly of eggs and toast, and that familiar scent sends a rush of guilt washing over me. Maya is in the kitchen.

I stumble to the bathroom, avoiding my reflection in the mirror because I know I won't like what I see. I splash lukewarm water on my face, but it does nothing for the weight in my chest. My mouth suddenly salivates and I can't find the toilet fast enough. Nearly missing completely, I manage to empty my stomach in quick fashion. I clean my mess off the seat and porcelain. The memory of last night is hazy, but not hazy enough. I remember the argument. The look on her face. The way she just gave up and went to bed without another word.

When I shuffle into the kitchen, Maya's already making breakfast. The light is soft, the morning sun filtering through the thin curtains, casting a golden glow over her. She doesn't look at me right away, just flips the eggs in the pan like it's any other day. I sit down at the table, the chair scraping loudly against the floor, and for a second, I half-expect her to snap at me, to tell me to make my own damn breakfast. But she doesn't.

Instead, she sets a plate of food in front of me—scrambled eggs, toast, and some avocado, sliced neatly on the side. My stomach churns, still sour from the night before, but the sight of it makes me feel something else. Shame. Undeserved kindness has a way of doing that to a person. I don't say anything, and she sits across from me, sipping her coffee, her fingers wrapped around the mug like it's an anchor keeping her steady.

"You okay?" she asks quietly, her eyes soft and a little sad. There's no anger in her voice, no edge to her words. Just concern. Pure and simple. She's too good for this. Too good for me.

I nod, though I'm anything but okay. The truth is, I don't deserve this moment, this calm. I'm still the guy who stumbled in drunk last night, who's been coasting through life and letting her pick up the pieces. She's been patient—too patient—and yet here she is, making me breakfast like it's nothing.

"I don't know how to..." I start, but the words die in my throat. Apologizing feels hollow. I've said sorry too many times.

Maya looks at me, really looks at me, like she's peeling back all the layers of avoidance, the excuses, and the screw-ups. And for a second, I feel like I'm transparent, like she can see straight through to the mess I've been trying so hard to hide.

"Devan," she says softly, "I know you've been struggling. I see it. But you're not this guy. You're better than this. You just have to believe it." Her voice is steady, filled with a calm certainty that I don't feel in myself. But the way she says it, the way she looks at me like she already sees the man I'm supposed to be... it stirs something inside me.

She believes in me, even if I've done nothing to earn it. She's still here, still making breakfast, still seeing something in me worth fighting for. And that snaps me out of it. It's not like a thunderbolt, but more like a slow dawning, like the fog in my head is beginning to clear, and for once, I don't feel like I'm drifting.

"Thanks," I mumble, knowing it's not enough but meaning it all the same.

She smiles, a small, tired smile, but it's real. And that's enough for now.

The drive to work feels brutal today. The air's colder, biting against my skin, almost mocking the dull ache in my skull. Every pulse of the hangover sends a sharp throb through my head, like my brain's trying to break free. But beneath the pounding, there's a strange undercurrent—something raw, cutting through the haze, though it does nothing to ease the pain.

I think about what Maya said, how she sees me as someone better than this. It's hard to believe, but for her to say that after last night—after everything—it's like she's offering me a lifeline. And for once, I don't want to ignore it.

I get to the office, bracing myself for Tom. The elevator ride up feels longer than usual, my heart thudding in my chest, and when I sit down at my desk, it's like I'm waiting for the axe to fall.

Tom calls me in almost immediately. His office is neat, painfully so, with everything in perfect order. The contrast between him and me is almost comical.

"Devan," he starts, his tone clipped. "I'm not gonna sugarcoat this. You're slipping. Missing deadlines, incomplete work, and yesterday—where were you? This lead for you to follow up on is starting to go cold."

I nod, swallowing the lump in my throat. His words don't sting as much as they usually do. Maybe it's because I already know he's right. Maybe it's because I've finally stopped pretending it's not a problem.

"I screwed up," I say, my voice surprisingly steady. "I know. I'll get the report and follow up on it today."

Tom eyes me, probably expecting the usual excuses, but I don't offer any. I'm tired of running. He sighs, rubbing the bridge of his nose. "Just get it done. We'll talk later."

I leave his office, the tension still lingering in my body, but there's a strange kind of calm underneath it. I sit down at my desk, the screen glaring back at me, and finally feel like I can focus.

The report, the assignment, it's about some local yogi—someone who's mastered the art of balance, both physically and mentally. They want me to interview him and write an article about how yoga has shaped his life. It feels ironic, given how out of balance my life is, but maybe that's why I've been avoiding it. Maybe it's time to stop avoiding things.

I pull up some different sites on yoga, reading through some quotes. Yogis talk about how yoga isn't just about the physical postures, but about finding peace within chaos, about centering yourself when life is anything but. As I read, something clicks, like my brain is finally catching up with what I already know.

Life doesn't stop being chaotic. It doesn't slow down for you to catch up. But maybe that's the point. Maybe it's not about waiting for the storm to pass. It's about learning to stand in the middle of it, calm and steady, while everything else swirls around you.

I've been running from the chaos, trying to dodge it, but maybe I've been doing it all wrong.

3

Sage of Wonder

Back at my desk, I start digging into the background of this yogi. His name is Raj, but in the local yoga community, he's something of a legend. Most yogis you picture are serene, calm, and peaceful—but Raj? He's different. He's led the kind of life that could inspire a Hollywood action movie, not just a wellness retreat.

From what I can gather, Raj started as a martial artist in his teens, training in disciplines I can barely pronounce. Then, in his twenties, he dove headfirst into extreme sports—rock climbing, skydiving, surfing in places where the waves looked like they could swallow whole ships. His body took a beating, too. There are stories of him shattering bones in remote places, only to somehow crawl back to civilization and heal himself. Over time, he got into yoga as a way to fix the damage he'd done, and somehow, it worked. Now, in his fifties, Raj is healthier, stronger, and more flexible than most people half his age.

He doesn't teach in studios or run flashy retreats. He's private, mysterious, offering one-on-one lessons to people who seek him out, like he's some kind of sage hiding on top of a mountain. You don't just sign up for his classes; you have to be recommended, almost like you need to prove you're worthy of his time. But those who do? They speak about him like he's changed their lives. I scroll through testimonials, reading about people who found peace, strength and confidence after training with him. Some even claim he saved them from themselves.

I look at my screen, then at the half-finished report in front of me and I feel a flicker of curiosity. Maybe it's because Raj seems so far removed from the life I'm living—while I'm barely holding it together, here's a guy who has not only pushed his body to its limits but has found a way to fix it, master it, and then transcend it. There's something about that I can't shake.

I reach for my phone and pull up the contact info my editor sent over. Raj's assistant answers after a couple of rings, and I half-expect to be turned away. But after a brief back-and-forth, she schedules an interview for the following afternoon. Just like that, I've got a time, a place, and a shot at talking to this elusive, legendary yogi.

As I hang up, I feel a strange sense of anticipation. Maybe it's because this is the first real assignment I've decided to care about in a long time, or maybe it's because something about Raj feels different—like there's something more to gain here than just an article.

I spend the rest of the afternoon reading more about him, diving into articles, interviews, and forums. Every story about Raj is like peeling back another layer of this guy who seems almost too good to be true. There are accounts of him hiking solo through the Himalayas, training under martial arts masters in Thailand, and even studying ancient healing practices in the Amazon. His life is a patchwork of adventure, risk, and recovery, and somehow, it all led him to this quiet, private life as a yogi.

By the time I'm wrapping up for the day, I'm more invested in this interview than I've been in anything in a long time. It feels weird, being excited about something for once. Maya is still on my mind, the argument from last night hanging heavy between us. I don't know what I'm hoping to get from Raj—maybe some insight on how to fix the mess

I've made of my life. Or maybe, it's just a distraction. Either way, I'm all in.

The next day, the air feels different. There's a crispness to it, like the season is shifting from summer to fall. I step into the yoga studio where I'm meeting Raj, a small, unassuming place tucked away from the bustle of the city. It's quiet here—almost serene—and the smells of incense and sandalwood greet me as I walk inside.

Raj is waiting for me in the corner. He's not what I expected at all. His hair is gray, tied back in a neat bun, and his eyes are sharp, intense, like they see everything without missing a single detail. He's wearing simple clothes—a loose, faded t-shirt and black pants—but there's a calm strength about him, something almost electric. His presence fills the room, even though he barely moves.

"Devan?" he asks, his voice smooth, with a hint of an accent that's hard to place. I nod, shaking his hand, and it's like shaking hands with a statue—solid, unyielding, but not rough. I immediately feel self-conscious. This man radiates discipline and purpose, two things I've been seriously lacking.

We sit down on cushions, cross-legged, facing each other in the middle of the studio. There's no desk, no chairs, no pretense. Just an open, quiet space. I set my phone between us to record the interview, but for a moment, I hesitate. Something about this feels different—more intimate than any other interview I've done before. I can't explain it, but I get the sense that Raj isn't just answering my questions; he's assessing me. Measuring me, as if to see if I'm ready to hear what he's about to say.

"So," I start awkwardly, clearing my throat, "I've been reading a lot about your life, and it's... well, it's incredible. The martial arts, the extreme sports, the adventures... But how did yoga become the thing that stuck?"

Raj smiles, a small, knowing smile, like he's heard this question a hundred times before. "Yoga is the practice that connects all of those experiences," he says. "It's not just about the body, though that's where many people start. It's about learning how to live in balance, no matter what chaos is happening around you. When I was younger, I was chasing adrenaline. But as I got older, I realized it was peace I was truly searching for."

His words hit me harder than I expected. *Living in balance despite the chaos.* It's like he's describing exactly what I've been failing to do.

"I think a lot of people are chasing something," I say, surprising myself with how personal it sounds. "But not everyone knows what that is."

Raj nods. "Most people spend their lives running from discomfort, from fear, from responsibility. But the real growth comes when you stop running. When you face those things head-on."

I sit back, letting his words sink in. He's not talking about yoga anymore, at least not in the way I thought he would be. He's talking about life—about the mess I've been making of mine. And somehow, without knowing anything about me, he's saying exactly what I need to hear.

The interview continues, and Raj talks about his journey, about how yoga helped him rebuild his body and mind after years of abuse. But the more he talks, the more I realize that this interview isn't just about gathering quotes for an article. It's becoming something else—something deeper.

Maybe it's about something I've been missing in myself.

Raj leans back on his cushion, his eyes narrowing as if he's carefully deciding how much to tell me. The studio feels even quieter, like the air itself is holding its breath. Then, with a deep, almost meditative inhale, Raj begins.

"Years ago, I was studying *Qi Gong* in the mountains of southern China," he says, his voice low and deliberate. "I had been training under Master Huang, an old kung fu master who believed that martial arts were not just physical—he taught that true mastery was the control of one's internal energy, one's *chi*. He was elusive, eccentric, and didn't take on students easily. But after years of proving my dedication, he began to teach me the subtleties of energy work, using *Qi Gong* to heal the body from within. It was… transformative."

I'm already hooked, hanging onto every word. But then Raj's expression darkens.

"It was during the final months of my time with him," he continues, "when the incident happened. One day, I was supposed to meet Master Huang near the peak of a mountain. The weather had been unusual all morning—thick clouds rolling in, the air heavy with electricity, like the sky was preparing for something violent."

His gaze shifts to the floor, as if reliving the moment. "As I climbed up the mountain path, the winds howled, and a storm broke loose—one of those storms where the rain is so fierce you can't see more than a few feet in front of you. Lightning was striking around me, the kind of strikes that don't just light up the sky—they tear it apart. But I kept going, determined to meet him. I didn't want to show fear."

Raj pauses, his fingers idly tracing the lightning scars that crawl up his wrists and neck. I hadn't noticed them before, not really. They're faint but unmistakable, like rivers etched into his skin.

"As I neared the top, I felt something—a shift in the air. It was as if the energy around me condensed into a single moment. Before I could even process it, lightning struck. Not just the mountain, but me."

My heart pounds just hearing it. I can almost feel the crack of electricity through the room.

"The bolt ripped through my body," Raj says, his voice steady but intense. "It was like nothing I'd ever experienced. Pain beyond imagining, but also… power. I lost consciousness almost immediately. When I came to, I was being dragged into Master Huang's small hut. He had seen it happen from afar and had come to find me. There was no hospital nearby, no modern medicine that could have saved me. But Master Huang didn't need any of that."

He stops, letting the weight of his words sink in. I'm completely absorbed, the image of Raj being struck by lightning playing out in my head like a movie.

"Master Huang performed a series of ancient healing techniques," Raj continues, "things I'd only heard whispers about before. He manipulated my *chi*, aligning the flow of energy in my body, keeping me tethered to life when I should have been dead. For hours, he worked on me, using pressure points, breathing techniques, and meditation. I don't remember much of it—just flashes of awareness, pain mixed with calm, like being suspended between life and death."

I swallow hard, trying to imagine what that must've felt like.

"When I finally woke up, I was weak, but alive. And something was different—inside me. The experience of being struck by lightning, combined with the *chi* work Master Huang did, changed me. I could feel energy moving through my body in ways I hadn't before. It wasn't just healing—it was as if I had been reawakened to the deeper currents of life itself. From that moment on, I became obsessed with understanding how energy could be harnessed—not just for myself, but for others. That's when I started studying Reiki and the deeper, more subtle arts of energy healing."

Raj's eyes lock onto mine, the weight of his story hanging between us. "Lightning didn't just scar me physically. It awakened something in me—a connection to energy that most people will never experience."

I'm speechless. I don't even know what to ask next. It's like I've been swept into something far bigger than just an interview. Then, without warning, Raj leans forward.

"I can show you," he says quietly. "But you must be open."

Before I can even respond, he grabs my wrists. His grip is strong but not forceful—there's no malice in it, just intention. And then, I see them clearly—the lightning scars. They climb up his forearms like jagged branches, pale lines that twist up toward his neck, disappearing beneath his shirt.

Raj begins to chant, his eyes closing, his voice low and rhythmic. The words are foreign, flowing in a melodic, otherworldly cadence. Sanskrit, maybe, or some other ancient language. I don't understand a word of it, but it doesn't matter. There's power in the sound itself, vibrating in the air between us.

At first, I feel nothing. Just the weight of his hands on mine. But then, slowly, I feel… something. A warmth. No, not warmth—something deeper. A pulse, almost electrical, traveling from his hands into mine, like tiny jolts of energy seeping through my skin. It starts in my wrists, then moves up my arms, spreading into my chest, my stomach, my legs.

With every chant, the sensation grows stronger, more intense. It's not painful, but it's overwhelming, like every cell in my body is waking up all at once. My breath catches in my throat, and for a moment, I feel like I'm on the edge of something—something vast, unknown.

Raj's chanting grows louder, more forceful, and with each syllable, the energy builds, pulsing through me like an invisible current. My head feels light, my limbs heavy, and I'm not sure if I want to laugh or cry. It's like being struck by lightning without the pain—just the raw, unfiltered energy of it. Suddenly, a vision ignites within me: a golden dragon ascending from the base of my spine, its shimmering scales radiating warmth and strength. I can almost see it, a magnificent creature rising above us, its wings unfurling like sunlit sails. It hovers protectively, bowing in reverence, as if honoring the sacred moment we've created together. In that instant, I feel enveloped by its power, a sense of safety and belonging that washes over me, grounding me in the chaotic energy swirling around us. The dragon's presence assures me that we are not alone—that I am a part of something greater, something vibrant and alive.

Then, as suddenly as it started, the chanting stops. All is quiet.

Raj opens his eyes and releases my wrists, the energy dissipating as quickly as it came. I'm left sitting there, stunned, my body buzzing like a live wire.

"What... what was that?" I manage to ask, my voice shaky.

Raj smiles faintly, his eyes calm, unbothered. "A reminder," he says simply. "That the power is always within you. It's always been there. You just have to learn how to harness it."

I sit there, still buzzing, my mind reeling from the experience. Whatever just happened, it was real. I felt it. I don't know what it means, or how to process it, but one thing is clear—this man, this yogi, is far more than just a teacher of poses and breathing exercises.

As I step out of the studio, his chant still echoing in my mind, a strange sense of contentment washes over me. In the fading light, I realize something within me has changed. I can't help but wonder.. what in hell just happened?!

* * *

Help Others Find Calm in the Chaos
Your Review Can Light the Way

"In a world full of noise, sometimes all we need is a quiet moment of peace."
– Alexander Morris

The world can feel overwhelming sometimes. But when we share something that helps, like a kind word or a helpful tool, we can make life a little brighter for someone else.

Would you help someone who's looking for balance in the middle of the chaos?

My goal with *Finding Balance in the Chaos* is to share simple ideas that can help anyone find a moment of calm, no matter how stormy life gets.

FINDING BALANCE IN THE CHAOS

But to reach more people, I need your help!

When someone is looking for their next book, reviews are often the first thing they read. Your review could be the reason someone decides to take a step toward peace in their life. It's quick, easy, and doesn't cost a thing—but it can make a big difference.

Your review might:

- Help someone find hope when they're feeling lost.
- Inspire someone to create healthier, stronger relationships.
- Encourage a person to pause and breathe when life feels too heavy.
- Be the push someone needs to start their own journey to balance.

If you want to help someone find the peace they've been searching for, simply scan the QR code below and leave a review. Your words could be the light that leads them through the chaos.

* * *

4

Flashing Intuition

Devan walked through the front door that evening with a strange, quiet energy bubbling beneath the surface. Normally, after a day like this—after an encounter like that—he would be bursting at the seams to tell Maya everything. He'd rush in, talking a million miles an hour, tripping over his words to get it all out. But tonight was different. Tonight, something had changed.

Maya looked up from the couch as he entered, her eyes soft but curious. She could sense it too, though she said nothing at first. Devan felt a warmth in his chest just seeing her there, her legs tucked underneath her, the gentle glow of a lamp illuminating her face. Instead of blurting out the surreal experience of the day, Devan simply smiled, a slow, gentle smile. He crossed the room, leaned down, and kissed her softly on the forehead.

"Goodnight, love," he murmured.

She blinked up at him, surprised by his calmness. "Going to bed?"

He shook his head. "No, I'm going to get some writing done."

Maya smiled, that smile that always made him feel more grounded, more present. "Alright. Don't stay up too late."

He chuckled softly, something like peace settling over him. "I won't."

In his small home office, Devan sat at his desk, the cool air from the open window brushing lightly against his skin. He opened his laptop and stared at the blank document. His intention was clear—he needed to write about his interview with Raj. He wanted to capture everything: the yogi's stories, the feeling of the energy coursing through him, the strange, electric connection that had left him buzzing for hours.

But as his fingers hovered over the keyboard, he began to feel it again—that warmth. The subtle pulsing that had started earlier in the day, ever since Raj had chanted those ancient words. Except now, it was growing stronger, spreading through his body like an electric current. Devan paused, his breath catching slightly as he became acutely aware of his own heartbeat, of the blood rushing through his veins.

He closed his eyes and tilted his head back, letting the sensation wash over him. The soft hum of energy wasn't just in his mind—it was in his bones, in every muscle, in every nerve. His feet, firmly planted on the hardwood floor, felt rooted, as if he were part of the earth itself, solid and unmoving. He pressed the tips of his fingers together, feeling the warmth in them, the tingle of life vibrating between them.

For a moment, he tried to focus on his writing again—he really did. But the sensation of energy surging through him was too overwhelming, too all-consuming. Devan exhaled slowly, sinking deeper into the feeling. His body was still, yet he could feel the movement within him—like a river of electricity coursing through his veins, lighting him up from the inside.

Then, something shifted.

It was like a flash of light, not outside him, but within. A sudden surge of knowing, a deep, intuitive wisdom from somewhere far beyond him. He couldn't explain it, but it felt as though time itself had folded in on him, showing him something ancient, something eternal. Devan's breath became deeper, slower, and almost without realizing it, he began to hum softly. The hum vibrated through his chest, resonating in perfect harmony with the pulsating energy inside him.

The hum grew, becoming more rhythmic, more intentional. Devan could feel his body subtly moving with the vibration—his shoulders swaying, his head tilting forward slightly, as if his entire being was aligning with something greater. And then, without even thinking about it, he began to chant.

It wasn't a conscious decision—his lips just moved, and the words, the sounds, poured out of him. It was the same mantra Raj had invoked earlier, the same ancient syllables that had vibrated through the air in the studio. Devan had no idea what they meant, but in this moment, it didn't matter. The words came from somewhere deep within him, and as they flowed out, the electricity in his body intensified.

His breath became the rhythm of the chant. His body, still rooted to the chair, began to feel weightless, as though he was floating, suspended in the air around him. The energy built and built until it was no longer just inside him—it was *him*. He *was* the energy, and the energy was everything. There was no separation between him and the world, between him and the stars, between him and time itself.

And then, just as suddenly as it had started, it stopped.

Devan blinked, opening his eyes to the soft glow of the early morning light streaming through the curtains. He could hear birds chirping outside, the gentle rustling of leaves as the morning breeze whispered through the trees. It was morning.

He stared at the light, his mind slowly catching up with the realization: he had been sitting there, in his chair, chanting and meditating… the entire night. But it hadn't felt like a night. It hadn't even felt like time had passed at all.

It was like a flash—a single bolt of lightning.

Yet, somehow, Devan felt more rested than he ever had in his life. His body didn't ache from sitting in the same position for hours. His mind wasn't foggy with exhaustion. Instead, he felt… *alive*. More alive than he had in years. His muscles felt strong, his breath steady and calm. His skin tingled with the warmth of life, as though every cell in his body had been recharged overnight.

Devan smiled, a soft, knowing smile. The answers he had sought, the energy he had needed, had come not from the outside world, but from within. He had tapped into something profound, something ancient and powerful, and it had transformed him in a way he still couldn't fully grasp.

Maya stirred in the other room, the quiet sounds of her waking up drifting through the house. But Devan wasn't in a rush to explain everything to her. For once, he didn't feel the need to blurt out everything in an explosion of words.

Instead, he rose from his chair slowly, deliberately, feeling the solidity of the ground beneath his feet. The day was just beginning, but Devan had already felt the energy of a lifetime pass through him.

5

Awakening

Devan stood in the soft morning light, feeling as if he had just tapped into an endless reservoir of energy. It was as though he had gained precious hours in his night of meditation, hours he could now reclaim in the form of movement and breath. With an uncharacteristic burst of spontaneity, he decided that today would be the day he finally went for a run.

Grabbing his phone, he set an alarm for 30 minutes—just enough time to feel the exhilaration of movement without losing himself in a daydream. As he set another alarm for brainstorming his article, a subtle thrill coursed through him. He could already feel the inkling of ideas swirling in his mind, waiting to be captured.

Before he could enen grab his shoes, he felt a surge of energy, like a radio tuning in to a perfect frequency. His body seemed to move on autopilot, guiding him through the motions as if he were three steps ahead of himself. In the kitchen, he was whisking together coffee for Maya and pouring himself a cup, all while slipping into push-ups on the floor, his muscles working effortlessly in harmony. It was a strange sensation, like his body was controlled by an antenna, receiving signals from somewhere far greater than himself.

As he stepped outside, the world enveloped him. The cool concrete beneath his bare feet was a shock at first, but then he felt grounded, as solid as a mountain. Devan tilted his face up to the sun, opening one eye, then the other, soaking in the golden rays as if they were a divine gift. He clasped his hands above his head, a silent salutation to the universe, inviting in warmth and light. Closing his eyes, he smiled inwardly, feeling a bright glow radiating from his heart—a calm, contented energy that made him feel rooted and connected to nature.

"Just breathe," he whispered to himself, feeling the air fill his lungs with cool crispness.

And then he was off.

At first, he ran with purpose, his feet striking the pavement in a rhythmic dance, but as he moved through the neighborhood, something shifted. The run transformed into a gentle stroll, each step more leisurely than the last. The aroma of coffee lingered on his tongue, a reminder of the warmth he had prepared for Maya. As he ambled along, morning critters greeted him—the fluttering of birds overhead, the rustle of leaves in the gentle breeze, and the soft scurrying of squirrels darting across his path.

Everything felt surreal, like the world was unfolding for him anew. The vibrant greens of the trees seemed to burst forth in a welcoming cheer, as if they were saying hello. Each sight was infused with beauty, the universe painting in colors more vivid than he had ever noticed before.

Devan's mind danced between thoughts and appreciation, sparks of wisdom igniting as he took in the cool air filling his lungs. He felt a deep connection with the world around him, as if nature itself was breathing right along with him. Every blade of grass, every flower petal, every gust of wind felt like an embrace, inviting him to surrender to the moment.

As he strolled, he marveled at how time seemed to slip away. The world blurred, and he forgot all about the alarms he had set. He was lost in the simple joy of being alive, enveloped by gratitude and wonder.

The gentle cadence of his footsteps matched the rhythm of his heart, each beat a reminder of his own existence. The sun warmed his skin, and he tilted his head back, allowing himself to bask in its glow, feeling the warmth seep into his very core.

Minutes turned into what felt like hours, and as he strolled past his own front door, a sudden jolt of reality snapped him back to the present. His phone alarm sounded, sharp and insistent, breaking the spell of appreciation that had enveloped him. He paused, staring at the door as if it were a portal back into his responsibilities and the hustle of life.

Right on time, he thought, the corners of his mouth curling upwards.

Devan felt alive, invigorated, and strangely ready for whatever lay ahead. He opened the door, greeted by the familiar scent of Maya's cooking wafting through the air, and he took a deep breath, filling his lungs with the promise of a new day.

The world outside had shown him the beauty of slowing down, of savoring each moment, he started to feel like he wasn't just coasting through life. He was living it.

As he stepped inside, he made a silent promise to himself: to hold on to this openness, this connection, and to embrace the journey ahead. He didn't know exactly what it would look like, but he felt ready to face it, one mindful step at a time.

6

Morning Ritual

MORNING RITUAL

Devan stepped inside, greeted by the familiar scent of Maya's breakfast wafting through the air. The aroma of sizzling eggs and fresh coffee filled the small kitchen, wrapping around him like a warm hug. Normally, the chaos of morning would have sent him straight to the couch, scrolling through his phone and nursing a cold cup of coffee. But today? Today felt different. Today was a promise of something new.

"Good morning, sleepyhead!" Maya called, her voice bright and cheerful. She was standing at the stove, her hair pulled back in a messy bun, a few strands falling free as she turned to give him a playful smile. It was a sight that never failed to warm his heart.

"Morning!" he replied, an uncharacteristic grin stretching across his face. "I'm going to take a quick shower before breakfast."

"Go for it! I'll have everything ready when you're done," she said, flipping a pancake with effortless grace.

Devan made his way to the bathroom, the excitement still bubbling within him. In the past, he would have waited for the water to warm up, enjoying the comfortable temperature before stepping in. But something inside him stirred. Why not dive right in? Why not embrace the moment? With that thought, he turned the faucet to cold, and icy water cascaded down as he stepped into the shower, a shocked gasp escaping his lips.

As he exhaled deeply, he felt steam rising off his body, almost like his very essence was igniting in defiance of the cold. The shock of the icy water jolted him awake, washing away the remnants of his groggy self, and instead, refreshing him with each drop that fell. It was invigorating, cleansing, and it sent ripples of energy coursing through him.

He finished quickly, feeling surprisingly alive, and when he stepped out, he caught a glimpse of himself in the mirror. The reflection staring back at him was different—more vibrant, more focused. For the first time in what felt like ages, he didn't see a slacker. He saw someone who was finally starting to wake up.

Feeling an unfamiliar sense of purpose, he moved through the bedroom and took a moment to make the bed. Normally, he would have stumbled out the door without a second thought, leaving the sheets a crumpled mess. But this time, he took his time, smoothing out the covers and fluffing the pillows. It felt good to do something simple yet meaningful, a small gesture of love and gratitude for Maya.

"Breakfast is almost ready!" she called again, her voice carrying a warmth that spread through him like sunlight.

When he joined her at the table, the sight before him was more than just food; it was a feast of colors and textures. Fluffy pancakes stacked high, golden eggs with just the right amount of seasoning, and crispy bacon that crackled with promise. As he sat down, he took a moment to appreciate it all, inhaling the delicious scents that danced through the air.

Maya poured him a cup of coffee, her hands steady, and as she set it in front of him, a warm feeling washed over him. "Did you make the bed?" she asked, surprised.

"I did," Devan said with a smile. "Wanted to show my appreciation for this beautiful breakfast."

This wasn't just a meal; it was an expression of her love.

"Thank you, baby. Little things like that mean the world to me," Maya replied.

Devan took a bite of the pancake, and it was like fireworks in his mouth. Each bite was richer than the last, bursting with flavor. He chewed slowly, savoring every morsel, and for a moment, he could feel the love she'd put into the food radiating through him.

"Wow, this is incredible," he said, glancing up at her, his heart swelling with appreciation.

Maya smiled, a soft blush on her cheeks. "I'm glad you like it. A good breakfast can really set the tone for the day, you know?"

Devan nodded, feeling a wave of gratitude. "Honestly, I think today's going to be a turning point," he said, surprised by the sincerity in his own voice.

"Yeah? What's on the agenda?" she asked, her eyes full of curiosity.

"I've got that article to wrap up, and I finally feel like I have some solid ideas," he said, excitement creeping in. "But it's more than just that. I don't know... I feel different, like I'm finally waking up."

"Good," she said softly, reaching across the table to squeeze his hand. "You've been stuck for a while, Devan. It's time you started owning who you are."

As they shared breakfast, Devan sensed a deeper connection between them, as if the meal had drawn them closer together in a way he hadn't experienced before.

7

Embracing Change

As the last bite of pancake disappeared, Maya finished washing the dishes and wiped her hands on a towel. "I should get going," she said, glancing at the clock. "I have that morning meeting with the team. But I'll be thinking about you today."

Devan felt a rush of warmth. "I'll be thinking about you too," he said, rising to meet her at the door.

She turned and he pulled her into a hug, wrapping his arms tightly around her. In that moment, the world outside faded away. Time seemed to stand still. It was just the two of them, enveloped in a cocoon of warmth and love. He breathed in her familiar scent—coconut and vanilla mingling with the lingering aroma of breakfast. The weight of his fears, doubts, and shame began to melt away as he held her close.

In their embrace, he felt a sense of safety and reverence. It was as if they were both donning armor against the chaos of the world outside. That's when he noticed something remarkable: a warm, bright hue surrounding them, almost shimmering. He had never known he could see colors like this, but now it felt like their energies were becoming magnified, radiant and alive. Basking in the soft white and pink aura that appeared to envelop them, he could feel the loving energy nourishing him with every breath.

"Don't forget to write!" Maya said, pulling back slightly to meet his gaze. The tenderness in her eyes made his heart swell.

"Of course my horse," he promised, planting a gentle kiss on her lips.

With a final squeeze, she stepped out the door, and Devan stood there for a moment, letting the essence of their connection wash over him.

Once the door clicked shut, he took a deep breath, the morning's energy still swirling inside him. He made his way to the living room and sat down at his laptop, determined to create an outline for his article. He opened a blank document and stared at the blinking cursor, feeling the weight of expectation settle over him.

As he tried to focus on the screen, the light irritated his eyes, and he felt an urge to close them.

What came to him wasn't the outline he expected, but a torrent of negativity that had been building inside. It poured forth, spilling onto the page as if it had been waiting for its moment to escape. His fingers flew over the keyboard, typing faster than he ever had before.

Everything that had gone wrong in his life.

He typed about the moments of anxiety at work, the arguments with Maya, the disappointment he felt in himself. The words flowed out of him like a raging river, each complaint cascading over the next, creating a torrent of truth that needed to be released. Over a thousand words poured out in mere minutes, and as he looked at the screen, he felt a burden lift. The negativity that had haunted him was finally documented, but it didn't feel like an end.

With his eyes still closed, he took a deep breath, allowing himself to sink into a moment of reflection. Suddenly, he felt a shift within him—a change in perspective. No longer did he want to embody the dark figure of complaint. Instead, he sought the voice of his best friend, his coach, his yogi sage, the part of him that saw beyond the chaos.

He closed his eyes again, and with every inhalation, he called upon that inner wisdom, allowing answers to flow out of him. This time, the words were different. They spoke of growth, resilience, and the path forward. They illuminated his fears, doubts, and insecurities, transforming them into stepping stones rather than barriers.

"Everything I've experienced has led me here," he typed, his heart racing with determination. The negativity he had just poured out became a distant memory as he harnessed this fresh perspective. He deleted the complaints and saved the positive affirmations in a folder labeled "The Good."

With his mind now clear and focused, he tackled the article about Raj. The words came swiftly, flowing from his fingertips like a stream of inspiration. He wrote about Raj's extraordinary life—his adventures, the lessons he learned, and the strength he found through yoga and energy healing.

In just ten minutes, he crafted a clear and comprehensive draft that felt like a true reflection of the man he had interviewed. As he looked up from the screen, expecting to see he was running late, he was astonished to find he still had almost an hour before he needed to clock in.

"Plenty of time," he murmured to himself, feeling a smile spread across his face.

Devan stood up, feeling lighter than air, and began to prepare for his day. He moved with purpose, a renewed sense of determination coursing through him.

8

Power of Observation

Laying out his clothes for the following day was something he'd never had time for before. Finding his keys, phone, and wallet felt seamless—almost effortless. Locking up the house, his actions coordinated in an order with purpose that he could anticipate. He was keenly aware of each step, each movement, each choice. As Devan settled into his car, the sun streamed through the windshield, warming his face and igniting a spark of energy within him. He took a moment to appreciate the world outside, where the morning was alive with promise. The city was waking up, and so was he. With a deep breath, he turned the key in the ignition and felt the engine purr to life beneath him. It almost felt as though the power from the engine was transferring energy through his feet, heart and palms. His pelvic floor tightened as he inhaled, sending the energy toward his crown. What a rush! The world around him, once chaotic and overwhelming, transformed into a symphony of little actions harmonizing into something beautiful. The drive to work had always been hectic and stressful, navigating through morning traffic and enduring the monotonous routine.

But today felt different. As he pulled out of his driveway and navigated through the neighborhood, he realized he was more present than he'd ever been. By becoming a powerful observer of his life, he managed to not drift aimlessly through the confusion of daily existence.

But just as he began to revel in this newfound awareness, he hit the morning rush hour. The cars ahead of him slowed to a crawl, and the familiar pang of frustration crept up. He clenched his jaw, ready to succumb to the familiar throbbing of impatience, but instead, he took a moment to breathe and placed his attention outside of himself. He felt as though he were looking at himself from the passenger seat and was completely removed from any emotions he would normally be having.

Glancing out the window, he spotted a little sparrow hopping on the grass beside a bench just off the road. It was a simple scene—just a small bird pecking at the ground, blissfully unaware of the steel and rubber maze of cars inching by. Devan felt a wave of appreciation wash over him. This fleeting moment, as minuscule as it seemed, would never happen again. He felt connected to the little visitor, as if the sparrow was a reminder of life's beauty in simplicity.

In that instant, he realized another truth. Looking to his left, past his physical body which appeared to be in a trance, he saw another driver erupting in frustration, banging on the steering wheel, face flushed with anger. He could feel that simmering tension radiating from the other car like heat waves rising from asphalt. He thought about the sparrow once more, observing how it seemed unfazed by the traffic, just watching the cars go by. It wasn't just about not getting caught up in the anger; it was about recognizing that anger wasn't a part of him unless he allowed it to be. Experiencing anger and irritation was like being stuck in the car in traffic. He could choose to stay stuck or he could sit on that bench on the side of the road watching the cars go by as carefree as the sparrow.

Just like that, as if on cue, the traffic began to pick up. The vehicles inched forward, and he felt a smile spread across his face. With one last glance at his feathered friend, he whispered a soft goodbye. "Adieu, little sparrow," he murmured.

He turned his attention back to the road ahead, feeling lighter, as if he had just shed a weight he didn't know he was carrying. The little moments, he realized, held immense power. With this fresh perspective, he could approach his day with a renewed sense of purpose and a heart open to the beauty that surrounded him.

The rest of the drive unfolded effortlessly, each turn and signal felt like a dance. Devan embraced this newfound sense of agency, eager to face whatever lay ahead. He had a mission—not just to write an article, but to weave the threads of his life into something meaningful, all while remaining anchored in the present.

Arriving at work, he took a deep breath, recalling the sparrow and the lesson it brought. Today was his day to soar.

9

Shifting Perspectives

Devan stepped back into the main office area, his heart still light from his morning practice. He felt centered, ready to take on whatever the day might throw at him. However, as he walked toward his desk, a voice broke the tranquility.

"Well, well, look who finally decided to show up on time," Alan sneered, a mockery dancing in his tone. His colleague leaned against the cubicle wall, arms crossed, wearing an exaggerated smirk that did little to mask the tension beneath it. "Thought we'd lost you to slacking off completely. Can't imagine why you still bother coming in if you can't pull your weight."

Devan could sense the stress emanating from Alan, thick and heavy. It was as if his own frustrations were being projected onto Devan, layered with an insecurity that radiated from him like heat from a flame. Normally, Devan would have mumbled under his breath and brushed off Alan's jibe as petty bullying. But today was different. He paused, letting the insult hang in the air creating a moment of uncomfortable silence for Alan before finally responding.

"Hey, Alan," Devan began, choosing his words carefully, "Are you doing ok? He said with compassion, "sounds like you've got a lot on your plate." He offered a soft smile, hoping to reach the man beneath the bravado.

Alan's sneer faltered for just a moment, replaced by a flicker of surprise. "Yeah, you know, it is what it is. I'm fine," he mumbled, but the way his eyes darted to the ground told Devan there was more to the story. Beneath the facade of bravado, Alan was struggling, battling his own demons, and Devan could feel it like a faint echo of his own past.

"Hold that thought, Alan," Devan said, surprising himself with the next words that flowed from his mouth. "Let's have lunch together. I was hoping you might be able to give me some tips on my latest article."

Alan blinked, taken aback. "Uh, sure, okay," he replied, the edge in his voice dulled slightly, as if he hadn't quite expected this turn of events. There was a moment of vulnerability in Alan's expression, a crack in his armor, and Devan couldn't help but feel a sense of hope.

After Alan walked away, Devan made his way to the bathroom. He needed a moment to collect himself, to let the unexpected interaction settle. As he stood at the urinal, he felt a familiar sensation wash over him, a mix of relief and that delightful little voice inside urging him to reflect.

He began to think about all the people who had made an impact on his life lately. As the sound of running water filled his ears, he closed his eyes for a moment, feeling the gratitude well up within him.

"I pray for Maya," he whispered, envisioning her radiant smile, the way she filled his world with warmth and light. "I pray for Raj, for the wisdom he shared with me." He thought of the sparrow he had seen that morning, hopping joyfully along the grass, embodying freedom in its simplicity. "I pray for my boss, Mr. Hargrove, that he finds the strength he needs to lead our team. And... I pray for Alan, that whatever he's battling, he finds peace."

As Devan emptied his bladder, he felt an incredible sensation of gratitude envelop him, a powerful force that seemed to amplify with each prayer. The awareness of his connection to others swelled in his heart, and he understood that this moment of reflection was an opportunity for something deeper.

Exiting the bathroom, he was surprised by how light he felt, as if he had shed a layer of tension along with his worries. The day continued on, but something subtle had shifted in the atmosphere around him.

As he settled back into his desk, he noticed Alan was no longer standing in his usual spot, but rather at his own desk, working quietly. And Mr. Hargrove, too, had approached him with a different energy, a hint of warmth in his tone as he complimented Devan on his improved punctuality.

"Good to see you're getting into the swing of things, Devan," Mr. Hargrove remarked, a nod of approval in his eyes. It felt like a small victory, but it was a step toward building a more positive environment at work.

Throughout the next hours, Devan observed the effects of his earlier prayers manifesting in subtle, yet profound ways. Alan, rather than sneering at Devan's efforts, seemed more engaged in his own work. When Devan caught his eye, he smiled—a genuine smile that broke the earlier tension.

The day rolled on, and Devan couldn't help but marvel at how this simple act of compassion had rippled through the office. It was as if each person he had prayed for had, in turn, become a little lighter, a little more open to connection.

By the time lunch rolled around, Devan and Alan met in the break room, their conversations shifting from tension to something more relaxed. Alan shared insights on writing that Devan found surprisingly helpful. They discussed their personal lives, sharing small tidbits that built a bridge between them.

As the clock ticked away, Devan felt a new sense of camaraderie growing—not just between him and Alan, but with everyone around him. It was the kind of energy that reminded him of the interconnectedness of all things, of how each act of kindness reverberated through the universe, like ripples in a pond.

And in that moment, Devan understood that life was not just about the articles he wrote or the job he held. It was about the people he encountered, the connections he forged, and the compassion he shared. As he finished his lunch and headed back to his desk, he felt invigorated by the knowledge that he was part of something larger, something beautifully intricate, and it filled him with hope.

10

A Chance Encounter

As Devan stepped out of the office and into the golden embrace of the evening sun, a wave of euphoria washed over him. The day had been transformative, each interaction adding a brushstroke to the canvas of his life. With a bounce in his step, he headed to the grocery store, determined to pick up some ingredients for a dinner that would show Maya just how much he appreciated her.

The entrance to the store loomed ahead, and just as he reached for the door, it swung open from the inside. There stood Raj, a radiant smile illuminating his face, his demeanor effortlessly gentlemanly. He was dressed sharply in a tailored peacoat that accentuated his athletic build, each movement exuding both elegance and strength. It was as if he had walked straight out of a magazine cover—polished and confident.

"Hey there," Raj said, his voice smooth and inviting. But it was not just the words; it was the way he carried himself. There was a depth to him, an enigmatic air that seemed to shimmer around him like an aura. He moved with a grace that reminded Devan of a well-crafted dance, each step deliberate and full of intention. He could feel the magnetic pull of Raj's presence, like the gravitational force of a star, compelling and impossible to ignore leaving Devan Speechless.

A CHANCE ENCOUNTER

In that fleeting moment, Devan passed him as if crossing a threshold into a new realm of awareness. No words were necessary; their brief exchange felt like an entire conversation. Raj's eyes sparkled with understanding, and his lips formed a subtle grin that communicated a sense of camaraderie. It was as though they shared a silent acknowledgment of each other's journeys, both vibrant yet complex.

Devan could hear Raj's voice echo softly in his mind, a soothing whisper of affirmation. Without moving his lips, Raj seemed to ask, *"How are you?"*

"Good," Devan responded silently, matching Raj's energy like they were in sync, vibrating on the same frequency. The exchange felt deep, like an unspoken bond had been forged in that brief moment.

Raj, still walking, gave a nod, his confident grin unwavering. *"That's the way to be,"* he responded, his words somehow reaching Devan's thoughts. Even as Raj exited the store, his positivity lingered, leaving Devan feeling unexpectedly lighter.

Devan stood for a moment, awestruck by the encounter. The brief interaction felt like a lesson in itself, an illumination of the possibilities that existed beyond mere words. He shook his head in disbelief, trying to wrap his mind around the depth of it all.

With a renewed sense of purpose, he stepped into the grocery store, shaking off the lingering connection with Raj. *Where's the spaghetti?* he thought, scanning the aisles.

He picked up a few ripe tomatoes and a loaf of crusty bread, envisioning the meal coming together. Grabbing the pasta, he headed for the wine section, choosing a bold red to pair with dinner.

At checkout, the cashier smiled warmly. "You look happy today."

"Thanks," Devan replied, smiling back. "I guess I just had a really good day." His mind still buzzed with the serendipity of it all.

11

The Journey Within

Dinner with Maya was more than just a meal; it was a ritual that spoke volumes of the love they shared. As they stood together in the kitchen, chopping vegetables and stirring sauces, Devan found himself enveloped in the familiar warmth of her presence. The aroma of garlic and herbs filled the air, blending with the soft music in the background, creating a sense of comfort and connection.

Maya spoke animatedly about her day—her voice rich with emotion, each word a thread that painted a picture of her experiences. She recounted the challenges she faced at work, the triumphs that lit her spirit, and the moments of laughter shared with colleagues. Devan listened intently, savoring the opportunity to hold space for her. He felt no urge to fix her problems or offer solutions; instead, he simply reassured her with nods and gentle affirmations, letting her know that she had a safe space to express herself.

As she talked, he poured them each a glass of wine, allowing the smooth liquid to flow like their conversation. He was grateful for this connection, realizing that listening was as powerful as speaking. It was an art, one he was beginning to master, and in doing so, he felt closer to

Maya than ever. Her laughter was a melody that resonated in his heart, a beautiful reminder of the joy they created together.

After dinner, the ever-familiar sound of silence settled in, wrapping around them like a gentle hug. Yet, within that silence, Devan could hear the voice of wisdom beckoning him, urging him to prepare for the journey that awaited him. He excused himself with a warm smile, knowing that the evening's reflection was only just beginning.

He stepped into the cold shower, the icy water cascading over him like a revitalizing waterfall. Humming softly to himself, he massaged Castile soap into his skin, the rich lather mingling with the chilled air. Each breath warmed him from the inside out, a simple act of meditation as he wound down from the day. The tension of life melted away, replaced by a profound sense of peace and serenity.

With each drop of water, he released the worries that had weighed heavily on his heart, sending silent prayers to his family, friends, and even to Alan, wishing them good health and happiness. Brushing his teeth, he transformed the mundane into a meditative act, each stroke a reminder of the care he wanted to extend beyond himself.

When he climbed into his freshly made bed, a wave of gratitude washed over him. He felt the satisfaction of that small act from the morning, recognizing its role in preparing him for the restful night ahead. As he settled under the soft sheets, the warmth enveloped him like a cocoon, inviting him to drift into a tranquil sleep.

Just as his eyes began to close, a thought sparked in his mind. If he could prearrange feelings in his waking state, why not create a signal to become aware while he slept? Raj had mentioned something about lucid dreaming during their interview, and it intrigued Devan. He imagined the little sparrow as his guide, a whimsical indicator in the dream world.

But it had to be extraordinary, something that would catch his attention amidst the chaos of dreams. He envisioned the sparrow in a tiny suit, flapping its wings as it demanded his report with a boss-like authority. Or perhaps, it would throw lightning like Raj, illuminating the dark corners of his subconscious. Even the idea of being trapped in a pink bubble with Maya, floating through the cosmos to collect love energy, made him chuckle.

All these vivid triggers seemed like excellent indicators that he was dreaming. If he could recognize them, he could become conscious in that dream state and take control of his journey. The more he contemplated, the more the possibilities unfolded like the pages of a book waiting to be written.

Once he settled on the right trigger, he felt the weight of sleep begin to pull him under. He slipped into a deep slumber, the little sparrow and its delightful antics dancing through his mind. As he found his consciousness flickering on the edge of the dream realm, the indicators he had created began to weave together into a lucid narrative.

He found himself standing in an open field, the ground beneath him smooth like polished stone, the sky above a swirling canvas of deep purples and blues.

His body moved on its own, guided by something beyond him. He felt his muscles engage, his limbs loose yet strong, as though they had known this rhythm all along. The air hummed with energy, and in the distance, faint echoes of Raj's voice guided him forward.

He began practicing martial arts like Raj, with fluidity and grace, each kick and punch a precise dance of strength and purpose.

As his movements flowed, he began to feel something deeper—his body twisting, turning, and soaring through the air as if he had taken on the shape of that beautiful golden dragon. In this state, he discovered what it meant to truly fly—not just physically, but in the realm of mindfulness and compassion. Devan soared across landscapes—mountains that towered like ancient sentinels, their peaks kissed by the clouds. He surfed waves that crashed against the shore, feeling the exhilarating rush of water and wind propelling him forward.

The sensation was transcendent, as if he were no longer bound by the ground, but flying with a powerful, unearthly freedom to wherever his heart desired.

Each ascent felt like a lesson, a journey of understanding and presence that filled him with joy.

The dream unfolded like a rich tapestry, and Devan reveled in the exploration, feeling as if he were learning to navigate not just the dream world, but the depths of his own soul. The act of flying became a metaphor for the freedom he craved in his waking life—a reminder that by embracing compassion and understanding, he could lift himself above the challenges that once felt insurmountable.

As he glided through the skies of his imagination, he knew this was just the beginning of a journey that would continue to expand and evolve. Each night held the promise of discovery, and with that thought, he surrendered to the sweet embrace of sleep, ready to learn and grow in ways he had never imagined possible.

12

The Stone and the Sand

Devan lay flat on his back, arms extended overhead, enveloped in a cocoon of pillows and blankets. The comforting embrace of his bed felt as snug as a bug in a rug, a perfect contrast to the dream that had just played out in the theater of his mind. He had drifted into a deep REM sleep, and now the remnants of that journey lingered in his consciousness like the fading notes of a beautiful melody.

In his dream, he had walked along a serene beach, the sound of gentle waves kissing the shore echoing in his ears. The sun had warmed his skin as he wandered, his feet sinking into the cool, damp sand. It was there that he had discovered a smooth stone, its surface polished by time and tide. Picking it up, he tossed it into the air, delighting in the way it spun and glimmered in the sunlight. But in an unexpected twist, he suddenly became the stone, plummeting through the air until a gentle giant caught him, lifting him high into the sky.

The sensation was exhilarating, a mix of fear and joy, as he soared higher and higher, only to be caught softly each time. It was a dance of trust, the giant's hands cradling him with care, until he would gently fall back onto the soft sand, returning to his original form. Each landing was a reminder of safety, of being held and supported, even in moments of uncertainty.

As Devan slowly awoke, he rolled onto his side, stretching out the various muscles of his body that had become stiff during the night. He felt the soft sheets beneath him, and for a moment, it was as though he was still on that beach, the sand cradling him in its embrace. The realization washed over him, profound and poignant. His dream was more than a whimsical flight of fancy; it held a deeper significance, a truth about life itself.

With each stretch, he took a moment to appreciate the comfort of his bed. He envisioned it as the warm, forgiving sand, supporting him and lifting him with each movement. As he felt his skin melting off his bones in blissful relaxation, a wave of gratitude surged through him. The connection to the earth and its elements resonated in his heart, echoing the lesson he had gleaned from his dream.

Like the stone tossed into the air, he understood that life was a series of fleeting moments. Just as the sparrow had danced on the wind, each experience was brief and beautiful, a reminder of the transitory nature of existence. We are here for only a short time, and it is in that impermanence that we find meaning.

The gentle giant represented a greater power, one that caught him in the air and assured him that he would be safe. Surrendering to this power was essential, a vital lesson he was beginning to comprehend. The earth, like the soft sand, was nurturing and protective, cradling him even in moments of chaos. In surrendering, he would find peace, just as the stone found solace in the warmth of the ground.

Devan closed his eyes again, letting the thoughts settle in his mind. He felt the love of the earth beneath him, as if he could feel the heartbeat of the planet itself. It was a reminder that they were all connected—humans, stones, sparrows, and the vastness of the universe. Each entity had its place, and he felt an overwhelming sense of belonging, as if he were a part of something grander than himself.

As he lay there, he remembered Raj's teachings about harnessing chi and the energy that flowed through all living things. He envisioned this energy as a current that connected him to everything around him, weaving an intricate tapestry of life. It flowed through the sand, the waves, the sky, and within him, each pulse a reminder of the shared experience of existence.

Devan took a deep breath, filling his lungs with air, and exhaled slowly, letting go of any lingering fears or doubts. He embraced the feeling of lightness, the buoyancy of trust that came from knowing he was supported by the earth beneath him. Today was a new day, a chance to live fully and embrace each moment as it came, whether soaring through the air or sinking back into the comforting embrace of the sand.

With that thought, he embraced his commitment to live mindfully, to appreciate life's fleeting moments, and to surrender to the beautiful uncertainty that lay ahead. Ready to greet the day with renewed vigor, he carried the lessons of the stone and the sand woven deep into his being.

13

Inner Radiance

Suddenly Devan sprang out of bed, feeling an undeniable surge of excitement coursing through his veins. He tapped danced around the side of his bed, the rhythm of his footsteps a joyful proclamation embracing his inner child. Today, he thought, he wouldn't trade this feeling for ten million dollars. The energy within him felt electric, vibrant, and alive.

Without hesitation, he jumped into the ice-cold shower, the shock of the water invigorating him like a jolt of pure energy. He reveled in the sensations, the cold droplets invigorating his skin and waking up every cell in his body. It was the earliest he had ever risen, but he felt ready to embrace the day with open arms.

After his shower, he downed a large cup of filtered water, feeling it wash through him, activating his insides and shaking off any lingering fatigue. Each action he took was deliberate, leading him toward greater feelings of joy and an overwhelming vibration that was both attractive and magnetic. He noticed that people around him were beginning to notice the change within him. There was a lightness in his step and an undeniable glow about him.

Throughout the day, Devan found pockets of time to stretch and breathe deeply, channeling his energy throughout his body. He focused on areas that felt tight or stagnant, visualizing the breath packing warmth and vitality into his facial connective tissues, inhaling confidence, strength, and compassion while exhaling pain, stiffness, and any emotions that no longer served him. It was a practice that felt transformative, the simple act of breathing becoming a ritual of renewal.

His interactions with his boss and coworkers shifted as well. Rather than being caught up in the chaos of office life, he actively listened, allowing them to express themselves fully. It felt good to be present, to hear their thoughts and feelings without the urge to interject or solve their problems. Each conversation became an opportunity for connection, a thread weaving him deeper into the fabric of his workplace.

During lunch, he took leisurely strolls outside, grounding himself in nature. He looked up at the treetops, acknowledging the sparrows flitting from branch to branch, and even the blades of grass seemed to communicate with him through the gentle rustle of the wind. Each moment in nature brought him closer to the profound awareness he had been cultivating.

Devan reflected on how poignant this awareness had become. In the past, he had dulled his senses by sacrificing his values, chasing fleeting pleasures while escaping the pain that had nearly defined him. Now, he understood the importance of being gentle with himself, much like the gentle giant who had caught him in his dreams. He realized that his alter ego, the confident and vibrant man he was becoming, was just as vulnerable as the stone being tossed into the air.

Knowing how easy it was to drop the stone, he recognized that it was equally easy to let go of anything in his life that no longer served him or aligned with his higher purpose. With each breath, he felt lighter, freer, shedding the burdens he had carried for far too long. His skin began to glow, radiating a magnetic presence reminiscent of Raj's captivating aura.

Devan understood that every action was an opportunity to practice—whether through self-care, creative visualization, meditation, affirmations, or prayer. How he lived his life determined his level of confidence and shaped how he felt about himself, projecting that energy into the outside world. As he cultivated this positive energy, it reflected back on him, creating a beautiful cycle of growth and fulfillment.

With a fresh perspective, Devan moved through the rest of his day with purpose and intention, each moment a chance to embody the joy and light he had discovered within himself. The world around him shimmered with potential, and he was determined to embrace it fully, step by step, breath by breath. He couldn't help but smile, knowing that he was on the path to becoming the best version of himself—a radiant beacon of light in a world that so desperately needed it.

14

The Unraveling

"Done!" Devan exclaimed as he rose from his desk, the hum of the office fading into a distant buzz. He had just completed his latest article on mindfulness, inspired by the insights he had gathered during his transformative journey.

But just as he was basking in the satisfaction of his work, he received a call from his boss, Tom.

"Devan, can you come into my office?" The tone was firm, leaving little room for interpretation.

Devan felt a knot form in his stomach as he made his way to Tom's office. He knocked lightly and entered, bracing himself for whatever was to come. Tom sat behind his desk, a furrow in his brow, the phone still in his hand.

"Have a seat." Tom gestured, and Devan complied, sensing the weight of the conversation ahead.

"Listen," Tom began, his voice steady but laced with disappointment, "we need to talk about your findings with the local yogi." He paused, letting the words sink in. "It turns out there are a lot of discrepancies here. The yogi you've been writing about—Raj—he's never even heard from you."

Devan's heart sank. "What do you mean? I interviewed him last week. I got some incredible insights!"

Tom leaned forward, his expression serious. "That's the problem, Devan. Phillip, the studio owner, called me up wondering if this interview was ever going to happen. He assumed it was canceled after never hearing from you. You've got some explaining to do."

Devan opened his mouth to protest, but Tom held up a hand. "Just let me finish. Everything in your article is about this 'Raj' character, and it didn't even dawn on me that wasn't his name until I received that call. I tried finding anything about this Raj, and I've got nothing. I've checked with the studio, and they're clueless about him."

"Wait," Devan said, his mind racing. "I mean, I did interview him! We had a great conversation—he shared all this wisdom about mindfulness and the power of presence. I—"

"Devan," Tom interrupted, "I have no problem if you want to write fiction or nonfiction, as long as it meets proof of concept. But I need you to keep me posted on the direction of your articles. This feels like you're working in the shadows."

The air thickened with tension, and Devan could feel the heat rising to his cheeks.

"On the other hand," Tom continued, shifting gears, "your article caught the attention of *The Urban Review*. They want to run an exclusive series on wellness bits focused on the power of mindfulness—something about finding balance in a chaotic world. Do you think you are up for the task?"

The sudden shift in the conversation knocked Devan off balance. His mind was still racing with the implications of his previous conversation. "*The Urban Review*? Really!?"

"Really," Tom confirmed, his tone softening just a touch. "But I need you to be transparent with me, Devan. If you want to pursue this opportunity, I need to know that you're not just spinning stories. Your integrity is on the line."

Devan nodded, a mix of excitement and apprehension churning inside him. "Of course, Tom. I understand. I'll clarify everything. I'll reach out to Raj again, get my facts straight, and make sure this is legitimate."

"Good," Tom replied, leaning back in his chair. "I want to see you succeed. But remember, this is your chance to shine. Don't squander it."

As Devan left the office, the adrenaline still pumping through his veins, he felt a surge of determination. He couldn't let this opportunity slip away. Raj had shared wisdom that had shifted his perspective, and he was eager to convey that to a wider audience.

But as he made his way back to his desk, doubt crept in. Had he imagined the entire encounter with Raj? The insights, the feelings of enlightenment—were they all just products of his own mind?

Devan took a deep breath, trying to ground himself but he needed answers. He had to reach out to Raj again. Whether it was real or a figment of his imagination didn't matter. He felt a calling to explore this further, to unravel the layers of truth behind his experience, and to bring that to his writing.

He quickly typed out an email to Raj, expressing his desire to meet again, to clarify the conversation, and to gather more insights for the article.

With each keystroke, he felt the excitement returning, the possibility of sharing Raj's wisdom with the world. The Urban Review wanted to run his series, and he wouldn't let confusion or doubt stand in his way.

15

Guiding Spirit

Devan was desperate to prove to himself that the encounter with Raj hadn't been a figment of his imagination. He retraced his steps, heading to the yoga studio where he had first met the wise sage. The memory of their interview was vivid, but something was off as soon as he arrived at the familiar address. Instead of the calm, sacred space where they had exchanged deep insights, Devan was met with the bright lights of a grocery store.

His heart sank.

He walked around the store in a daze, scanning the aisles, searching for some sign of Raj, some clue that this strange reality was just a mistake. But the studio was gone. In its place, nothing but canned goods, fresh produce, and oblivious shoppers. The memory of running into Raj at the grocery store came flooding back—was it here where they'd met? Was that the real interaction?

None of this made sense.

Over the following weeks, Devan tried everything he could to track Raj down. He called the phone numbers he had found, visited websites that had once pointed to the yoga studio, but everything had changed, as if someone had rewritten the entire narrative. All traces of Raj had vanished. No one at the studio had heard of him, and no one could explain the sudden shift.

Devan's confusion grew by the day. Was this a cosmic joke? A dream he hadn't woken from? He was starting to question his sanity. How could someone like Raj—so vibrant and real—simply disappear from existence?

As the days ticked closer to his interview with *The Urban Review*, Devan knew he couldn't let this bizarre series of events sabotage his opportunity. This was the chance of a lifetime, and he was determined to show up, even if the mystery of Raj remained unresolved. After all, if he could write fiction or nonfiction, maybe he could incorporate this strange, almost otherworldly experience into his future work. Perhaps this was meant to be part of his journey.

Devan steeled himself, deciding to let go of his obsessive need for answers and instead surrender to the eerie events that had unfolded. It was unnerving, but in a way, it was liberating. There was something here—a lesson he hadn't yet grasped—and he was willing to trust that it would reveal itself in time.

On the day of his interview, Devan arrived at *The Urban Review* headquarters, nervous and slightly frazzled. He had dressed sharply, but the swirling thoughts of his encounter with Raj still danced in the back of his mind. He couldn't shake the feeling that something bigger was happening, something he couldn't yet see.

As he waited in the lobby, he glanced around at the pictures that lined the walls. There were photos of Mr. Bodhi, his soon-to-be employer, in incredible situations—skydiving over tropical islands, standing beside the Dalai Lama, exploring ancient ruins. It was clear that this man had lived several lifetimes, each one more adventurous than the last.

A voice pulled him out of his thoughts. "Mr. Bodhi will see you now," the secretary announced.

Devan stood, his heart pounding in his chest. As he entered the office, a sense of familiarity washed over him. The air was thick with the scent of sandalwood, and the atmosphere held an almost mystical quality. He took a deep breath, steadying himself as he crossed the threshold.

Behind the large mahogany desk sat a tall figure, his back to the door. Devan could only see his hands, folded behind his head, his legs crossed leisurely. There was an unmistakable air of mystery and power in the room, like he had stepped into another world.

The chair slowly turned to reveal Mr. Bodhi, a grin spreading across his face. "Devan! How's it goin'?" he said, his voice warm and casual.

Devan froze. The voice, the energy, the presence—it felt like Raj was staring right at him.

He couldn't believe it. This was the man he had interviewed, the same person who had imparted all that wisdom. But how? Why was he here, now posing as his new employer?

All Devan could muster in response was, "Good." His mind raced as the words came out automatically.

"That's the way to be," Mr. Bodhi replied, the same auspicious phrase Raj had used sent a chill up his spine. It was like a switch had been flipped, and suddenly, everything clicked into place.

Devan felt a wave of realization wash over him. Raj hadn't disappeared. He was right in front of him, hidden in plain sight, perhaps guiding him all along. The synchronicity, the lessons, the bizarre unfolding of events—it all made sense now. Raj wasn't just a yogi. He was something much more—someone with a deeper purpose, a mentor playing multiple roles in Devan's life.

As they began their conversation, Devan found himself not just being interviewed, but being taught. Every question Mr. Bodhi asked had layers of meaning, every statement seemed designed to push Devan further along his path.

By the end of the meeting, Devan felt an overwhelming sense of excitement. He had been chasing answers, but the truth had been with him the entire time. Raj—Mr. Bodhi—was a guide, helping him to unlock the power within himself, helping him find his own voice and purpose. And now, he was being given a platform to share that with the world.

As Devan left the office, a smile played on his lips. The mystery of Raj may never be fully explained, but he no longer needed an explanation. Some things were meant to remain enigmatic, pushing him forward on his journey toward understanding.

And with *The Urban Review* series ahead of him, he knew his next adventure was right around the corner.

* * *

Finding Balance in the Chaos

I hope that you've gleaned some techniques to find calm in the middle of life's storms, it's time to share what you've learned. By leaving a review, you can help other readers find the same peace and balance you've experienced.

Sharing your honest opinion on Amazon not only helps others decide if this book is right for them but also spreads the message of mindfulness and balance to those who need it most.

Thank you for being a part of this journey. Balance grows when we share what we've learned—and with your help, others can find their own path to calm.

Scan the QR Code below to leave your review on Amazon.

GUIDING SPIRIT

Afterword

As we reach the end of Finding Balance in the Chaos, *I want to take a moment to thank you for joining Devan on his journey of self-discovery and transformation. My hope is that this book has offered you not just a story, but also inspiration and practical insights that you can carry into your own life. I encourage you to reflect on your experiences as you read and to embrace the lessons that resonate with you.*

I would love to hear your stories of transformation—whether they are small moments of clarity or significant changes in perspective. Your journeys are important, and sharing them can foster a sense of community and connection among us all. If you found value in this book, I kindly ask that you leave an honest review and share it with your friends and family. Your support means the world to me and helps others discover the messages within these pages.

Thank you for being a part of this experience. I look forward to sharing more with you in future publications, and I hope our paths continue to intersect as we navigate the beautiful chaos of life together.